Reconstruction
FREEDOM DELAYED

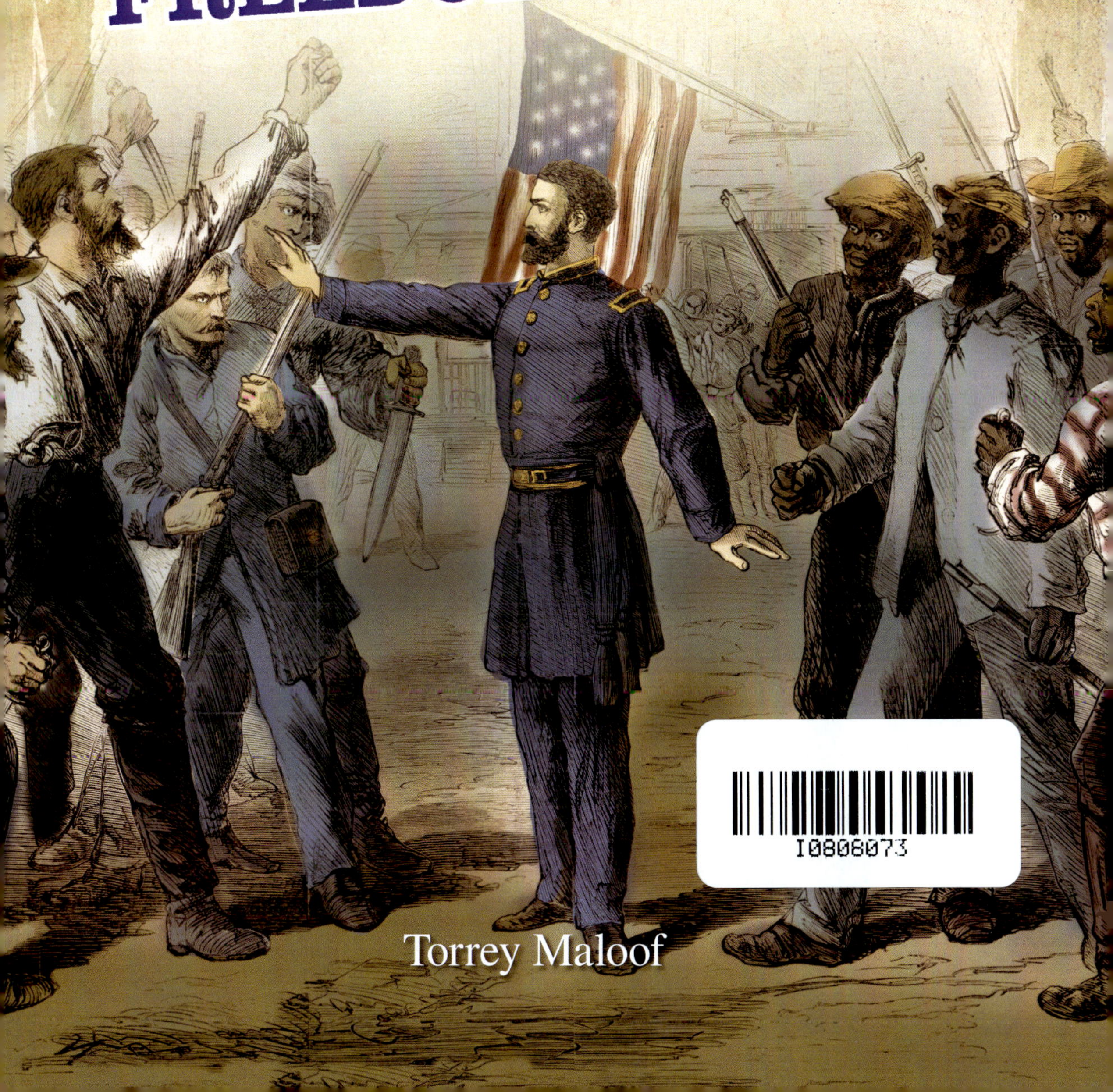

Torrey Maloof

Consultants

Vanessa Ann Gunther, Ph.D.
Department of History
Chapman University

Nicholas Baker, Ed.D.
Supervisor of Curriculum and Instruction
Colonial School District, DE

Katie Blomquist, Ed.S.
Fairfax County Public Schools

Publishing Credits

Rachelle Cracchiolo, M.S.Ed., *Publisher*
Conni Medina, M.A.Ed., *Managing Editor*
Emily R. Smith, M.A.Ed., *Series Developer*
Diana Kenney, M.A.Ed., NBCT, *Content Director*
Courtney Patterson, *Senior Graphic Designer*
Lynette Ordoñez, *Editor*

Image Credits: Cover and p. 1 LOC [LC-USZ62-105555]; p. 5 LOC [LC-DIG-ppmsca-19233]; p. 6 LOC [lprbscsm.scsm0283]; p. 7 LOC [LC-DIG-ppmsca-33069]; p. 8 Ms1992-003; Robert Taylor Preston Papers, 1849-1871, Special Collections, University Libraries, Virginia Polytechnic Institute and State University; p. 10 Courtesy of Louisiana State University Libraries Special Collections; pp. 11, 21 North Wind Picture Archives; p. 14 (top) LOC [LC-DIG-ppmsca-39591]; p. 14-15 LOC [LC-DIG-ppmsca-39592]; p. 15 Courtesy of Michael Mahler; p. 16 LOC [LC-USZ62-32499]; p. 17 NARA [1943528]; p. 18 Bettmann/Getty Images; p. 19 LOC [LC-USZ62-98798]; pp. 20, 32 Sarin Images/Granger, NYC; p. 21 North Wind Picture Archives; p. 22 LOC [LC-USZ62-57339]; p. 23 LOC [LC-DIG-pga-02595]; p. 24 (left) LOC [LC-USZ62-89311], (bottom) LOC [LC-DIG-ppmsca-15785]; p. 25 LOC [LC-DIG-ds-04504]; p. 26 (top) LOC [LC-DIG-ppmsca-38818], (bottom) LOC [LC-USZ62-60139]; p. 27 LOC [LC-DIG-det-4a13432]; p. 28 LOC [LC-DIG-ppmsca-37947]; pp. 29 LOC [LC-DIG-ppmsca-34808]; p. 32 Sarin Images/Granger, NYC; back cover LOC [LC-DIG-ds-04504]; all other images from iStock and/or Shutterstock.

Library of Congress Cataloging-in-Publication Data

Names: Maloof, Torrey, author.
Title: Reconstruction : freedom delayed / Torrey Maloof.
Description: Huntington Beach, CA : Teacher Created Materials, 2017. |
Includes index.
Identifiers: LCCN 2016034226 (print) | LCCN 2016038169 (ebook) | ISBN
9781493838066 (pbk.) | ISBN 9781480757714 (eBook)
Subjects: LCSH: Reconstruction (U.S. history, 1865-1877)--Juvenile literature. | Southern States--History--1865-1877--Juvenile literature. |
Southern States--Social conditions--1865-1945--Juvenile literature. | United States--History--1865-1898--Juvenile literature. | United States--Race relations--19th century--Juvenile literature. | United States--Social conditions--1865-1918--Juvenile literature.
Classification: LCC E668 .M33 2017 (print) | LCC E668 (ebook) | DDC 973.8--dc23
LC record available at https://lccn.loc.gov/2016034226

Teacher Created Materials
5301 Oceanus Drive
Huntington Beach, CA 92649-1030
http://www.tcmpub.com

ISBN 978-1-4938-3806-6

Table of Contents

At the War's End

The audience roars with laughter. The play *Our American Cousin* is being performed. The comedy, featuring an uncouth and awkward American man meeting his refined British relatives, proves to be a big hit with the crowd. Again, laughter fills the packed theatre. Amidst the merriment, a boy sees a man leap from a balcony and land on the stage. The man shouts in Latin, "Sic semper tyrannis," then runs off the stage. The boy is confused and frightened. The crowd's laughter quickly turns to screams of horror.

Booth jumps onto the stage after assassinating Lincoln.

Lincoln's death

It was on that night, April 14, 1865, that John Wilkes Booth entered a private box above the stage at Ford's Theatre. He held a pistol to President Lincoln's head and fired. The shot proved fatal. Lincoln died the following morning, leaving a nation in turmoil. General Lee had surrendered six days earlier. The Civil War was ending. Now, the war-torn United States faced the daunting task of rebuilding and healing its wounds without its courageous leader.

SAY WHAT?

"Sic semper tyrannis" is Latin for "thus always to **tyrants**." Booth was a Southern sympathizer. He thought of Lincoln as a tyrant. He felt that the president was out to destroy his beloved South.

Different Plans

Even before the war had ended, President Lincoln was thinking about how to unite the nation once the fighting ceased. His main goal was always to bring the Southern states back into the **Union**. But, what was the best way to do this? He didn't want to punish the South. He wanted reconciliation. The majority of the fighting had taken place in the South. As a result, the area was destroyed. Cities were in ruins. Fields and farms were burned until nothing remained. The South needed to be rebuilt. It needed to be reconstructed. Lincoln devised a plan.

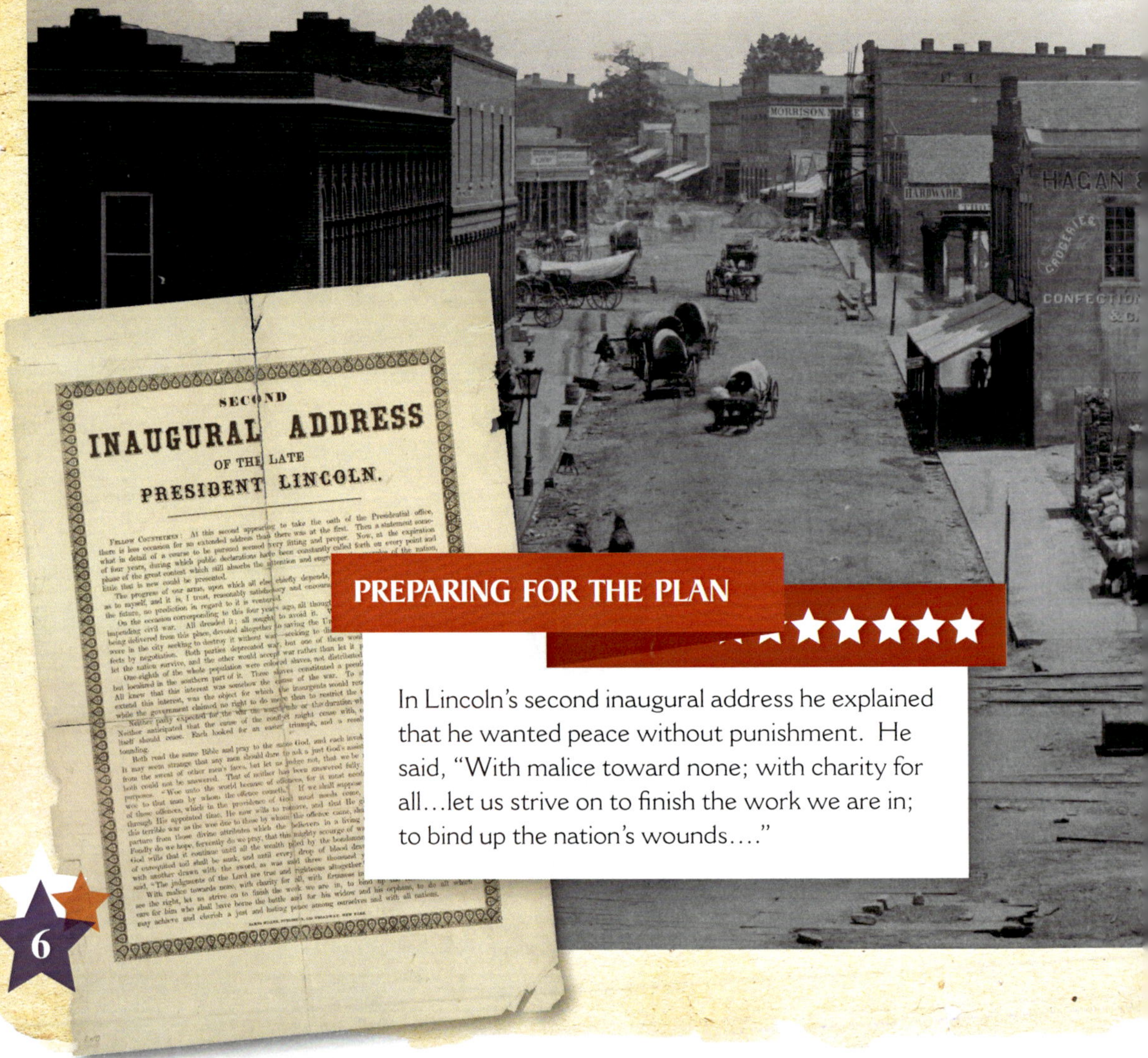

PREPARING FOR THE PLAN

In Lincoln's second inaugural address he explained that he wanted peace without punishment. He said, "With malice toward none; with charity for all…let us strive on to finish the work we are in; to bind up the nation's wounds…."

There were three main points in Lincoln's plan for Reconstruction. First, all Southerners, except high-ranking military leaders, would be granted a full **pardon**. All their property would be restored to them, except for the people they enslaved who were now free. The second point explained how a Southern state could rejoin the Union. To do this, 10 percent of its voters had to swear allegiance to the Union. The state also had to agree to outlaw slavery. After a new state government and constitution had been established, the state would then be readmitted. Lastly, Lincoln wanted Southern states to make plans to help formerly enslaved people adjust to freedom. However when Lincoln died, the plan changed.

Atlanta in ruins during the Civil War

Following Lincoln's death, Andrew Johnson was sworn in as the 17th president. Johnson had a different plan for Reconstruction. He favored stronger state governments. He believed that Southern states should make their own decisions about how to rebuild. Johnson was from the South. So he was more sympathetic. He granted pardons to everyone, even military leaders and officials. Johnson did very little for the wellbeing of freed slaves. He showed no interest in protecting them, giving them rights, or helping them adjust to their new lives. Johnson called his plan Restoration. This meant he wanted to restore the country back to the way it was.

ANDREW JOHNSON,
PRESIDENT OF THE UNITED STATES OF AMERICA,
TO ALL TO WHOM THESE PRESENTS SHALL COME, GREETING:

Whereas, R. T. Preston, of Montgomery County, Virginia, by taking part in the late rebellion against the Government of the United States, has made himself liable to heavy pains and penalties;

And whereas, the circumstances of his case render him a proper object of Executive clemency;

Now, therefore, be it known, that I, ANDREW JOHNSON, President of the United States of America, in consideration of the premises, divers other good and sufficient reasons me thereunto moving, do hereby grant to the said R. T. Preston a full pardon and amnesty for all offences by him committed, arising from participation, direct or implied, in the said rebellion, conditioned as follows:

1st. This pardon to be of no effect until the said R. T. Preston shall take the oath prescribed in the Proclamation of the President … May 29th, 1865.

pardon signed by Johnson

Andrew Johnson

BEG FOR YOUR PARDON

Johnson grew up poor. He resented the rich Southern landowners. He wanted them to beg for their pardons. So, Johnson made high-ranking military officials and the wealthy personally ask him for their pardons.

This 1867 cartoon shows President Johnson as "King Andy."

Members of Congress did not like Johnson's plan. They saw that it was not working. They heard reports of Southerners abusing African Americans. Riots were breaking out in the South. Congress felt the government needed to play a stronger role in Reconstruction. They pushed for harsher punishment and more restrictions for the South. But, the president did not agree. He did not care what Congress thought. During this time, people started to call the president King Andy because, like a king, he ran the country how he pleased. Congress was forced to battle with Johnson throughout the Reconstruction era.

Freedmen's Bureau

Four million **freedmen** were now starting new lives. They needed to adjust to a life of freedom and independence. This meant finding jobs and homes. They needed food and clothing. The road was not an easy one to travel. They faced **prejudice** (PREJ-uh-dis) and **racism** at every turn. To help in this time of transition, Congress created the Freedmen's **Bureau** (BYOOR-oh).

newly freed African Americans in Richmond, Virginia, in 1865

Lost Friends.

[We make no charge for publishing these letters from subscribers. All others will be charged fifty cents. Pastors will please read the requests published below from their pulpits, and report any case where friends are brought together by means of letters in the SOUTHWESTERN.]

DEAR EDITOR—I wish to inquire for my son. His name is Hannibal Harris. When I left him he was in Kentucky. He was only three years old. He belonged to Mr Sylvester Harris. His father belonged to John Woodforks. My name was Winnie Smith. Then I married Reuben Harris. I would be happy to learn his whereabouts. My name and address is Winnie Chapman, care Rev. G. W. Smith, between K and L 31st st[...] veston, Texas.

A woman places an ad in a Louisiana newspaper in hopes of finding her son.

REUNITED

Slave owners often tore families apart when they sold enslaved people. Bureau agents tried to help African Americans find their family members. They placed ads in newspapers and searched records in an attempt to reunite them.

The Freedmen's Bureau opened offices across the South. Its mission was to give former slaves the tools and skills needed to care for themselves. It gave out food, clothing, and medical care to help African Americans survive until they could stand firmly on their own feet. The bureau built hospitals in which they treated more than 450,000 patients. It started schools to educate African Americans. It trained them to become teachers. It helped men find work and sign labor contracts.

Bureau agents tried to make sure African Americans were treated fairly by white Southerners. But, that was not an easy task. Many white Southerners resisted the bureau's efforts. They saw the agents as enemies. They didn't want to accept the fact that slavery had ended. Some agents even faced threats and violence. But, they were determined to help.

Freed African Americans wed in 1870.

MASS MARRIAGES

Slave marriages were not legal in the eyes of the government. When slavery was abolished, African Americans longed to make their marriages legal. The bureau held mass weddings for dozens of couples at a time.

Unfair Treatment

While the Freedmen's Bureau tried its best to help and protect African Americans during Reconstruction, it was not always successful. Many white Southerners would stop at nothing to return to their old way of life. They did not want African Americans to be free. And they most certainly did not want them to have equal rights.

This 1868 political cartoon shows the head of the Freedmen's Bureau between angry groups of African Americans and white people.

Black Codes

After the Civil War, Southern states created black codes. These were state laws that limited the freedom of African Americans. They were not allowed to serve on juries. Voting was prohibited. In some states, freedmen could not testify against white people in a court of law or own guns. And they had to obey **curfews**. Some states banned African Americans from owning or renting land. There were laws that stated they could only work as farmers or servants for white families. If African Americans could not prove that they had jobs, they could be arrested and thrown in jail. These laws were meant to make African Americans feel enslaved again. The South had found a loophole. It was instituting a new form of slavery. And it was doing so within the realm of the Constitution.

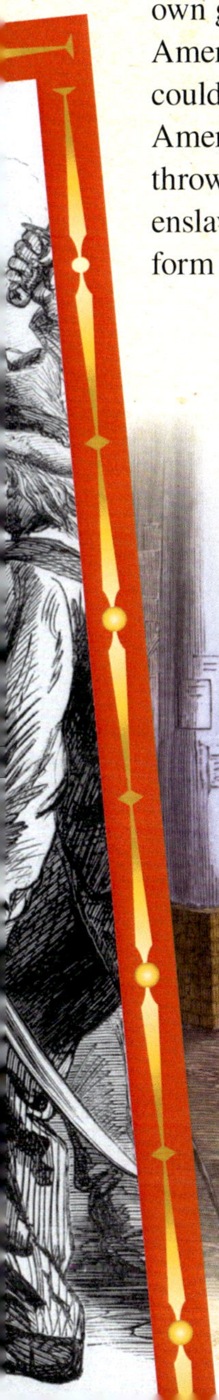

One black code allowed a freedman's services to be sold to pay his debts.

Sharecropping

The Civil War ended in the spring, meaning it was time to plow and plant seeds for the next harvest. Prior to the war, enslaved people would have done all this work, but now they were free. Landowners faced a big problem. They needed workers, and they needed them fast. However, after the war, landowners had no money to pay laborers. Their solution was sharecropping.

sharecropper home

Sharecropping was a system in which a worker signed a contract with a landowner. The landowner supplied the worker, almost always a former slave, with a cabin, a plot of land, and a mule. Some food, seeds, and tools were provided, as well. At the end of the year, the worker had to "share" the crops produced with the landowner. But it was not a fair system. The contracts stated that the worker could keep only about one-third of the crop. The worker then had to sell that small amount in order to repay the landowner for using the land, cabin, food, and tools. Almost every worker ended up in debt.

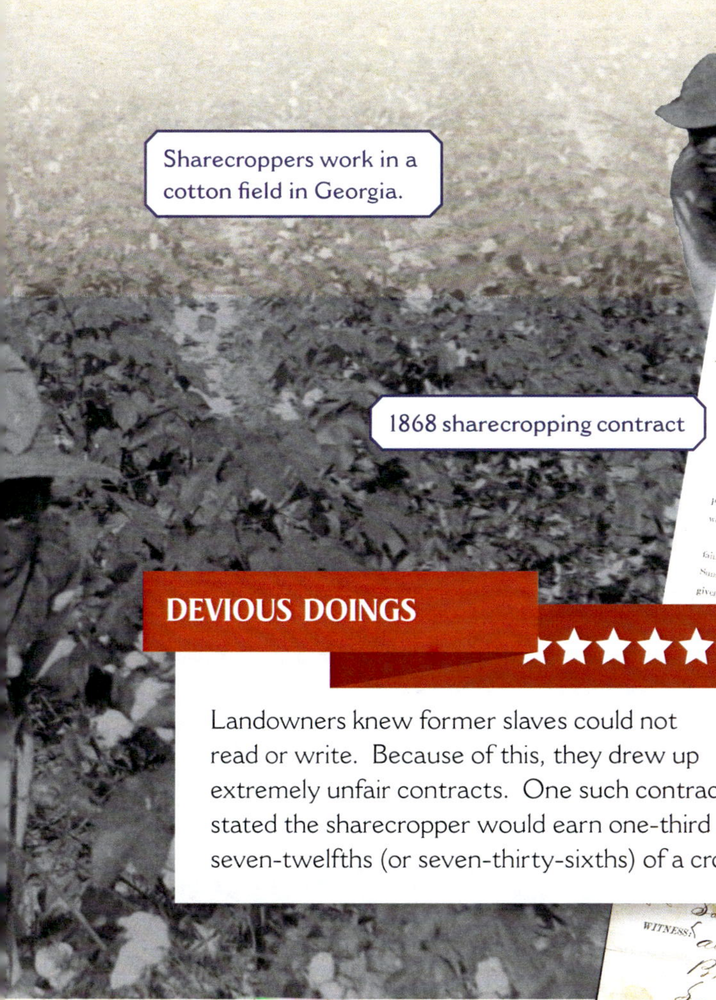

Sharecroppers work in a cotton field in Georgia.

CONTRACT FOR LABOR.

State of Alabama,

1868 sharecropping contract

DEVIOUS DOINGS

Landowners knew former slaves could not read or write. Because of this, they drew up extremely unfair contracts. One such contract stated the sharecropper would earn one-third of seven-twelfths (or seven-thirty-sixths) of a crop!

Congress Fights Back

Congress had enough of Johnson's Reconstruction plan. It was time to fight back and end the black codes. They wanted to give civil rights to African Americans. In April of 1866, Congress passed a civil rights act. It gave citizenship and rights to all males (except American Indians), "of every race and color, without regard to any previous condition of slavery." Johnson **vetoed** the bill. But Congress overturned the veto. The bill became a law. This was an important first step.

In 1867, Congress passed the First Reconstruction Act. Johnson vetoed it, too. But once again, Congress overturned his veto. This act called for the South to be broken into five military districts. U.S. troops would occupy each district and enforce laws to protect African Americans. Congress also placed certain demands on the South. They had to elect new leaders. These leaders would rewrite state constitutions. The states also had to **ratify** the 14th Amendment. Only then, could a Southern state rejoin the Union.

The next year, Congress overturned another veto to pass the Second Reconstruction Act. This act put troops in charge of voter registration to make sure it was fair.

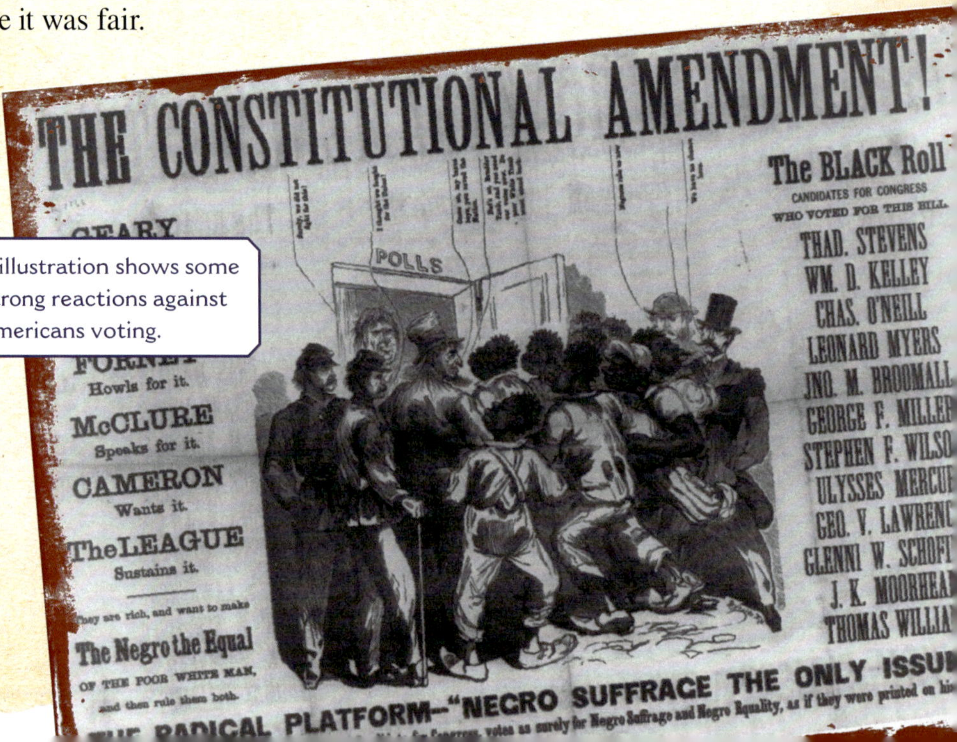

This 1868 illustration shows some people's strong reactions against African Americans voting.

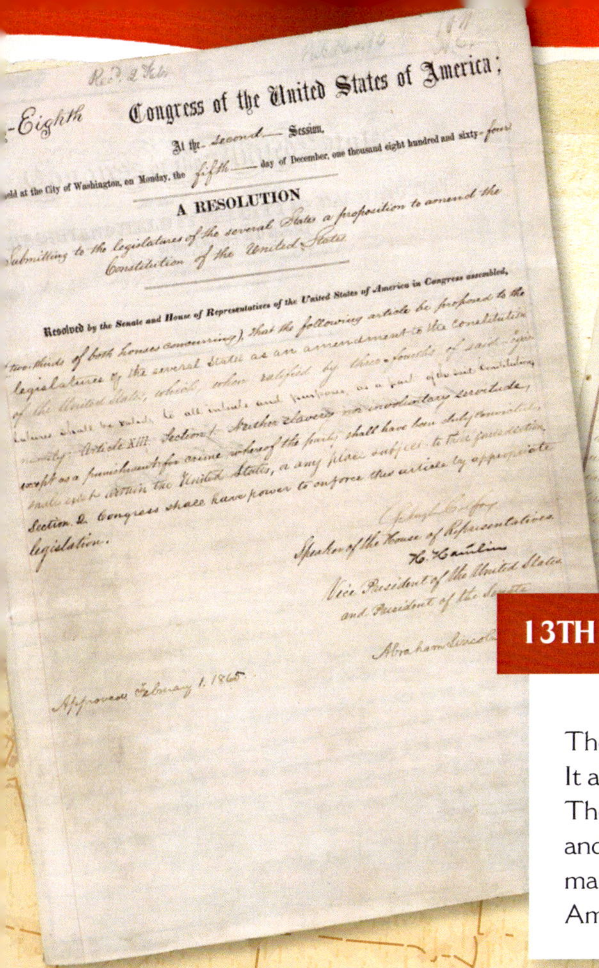

-Eighth Congress of the United States of America;

At the Second Session,

eld at the City of Washington, on Monday, the fifth day of December, one thousand eight hundred and sixty-four

A RESOLUTION

Submitting to the legislatures of the several States a proposition to amend the Constitution of the United States.

Resolved by the Senate and House of Representatives of the United States of America in Congress assembled, (two-thirds of both houses concurring), that the following article be proposed to the legislatures of the several States as an amendment to the constitution of the United States, which, when ratified by three-fourths of said legislatures shall be valid, to all intents and purposes, as a part of the said Constitution, namely: Article XIII. Section 1. Neither slavery nor involuntary servitude, except as a punishment for crime whereof the party shall have been duly convicted, shall exist within the United States, or any place subject to their jurisdiction. Section 2. Congress shall have power to enforce this article by appropriate legislation.

Schuyler Colfax
Speaker of the House of Representatives.
H. Hamlin
Vice President of the United States and President of the Senate
Abraham Linco

Approved February 1. 1865.

13TH AND 14TH AMENDMENTS

The 13th Amendment was ratified in 1865. It abolished slavery in the United States. The 14th Amendment granted citizenship and the rights that came with it to every man born in the United States, except American Indians.

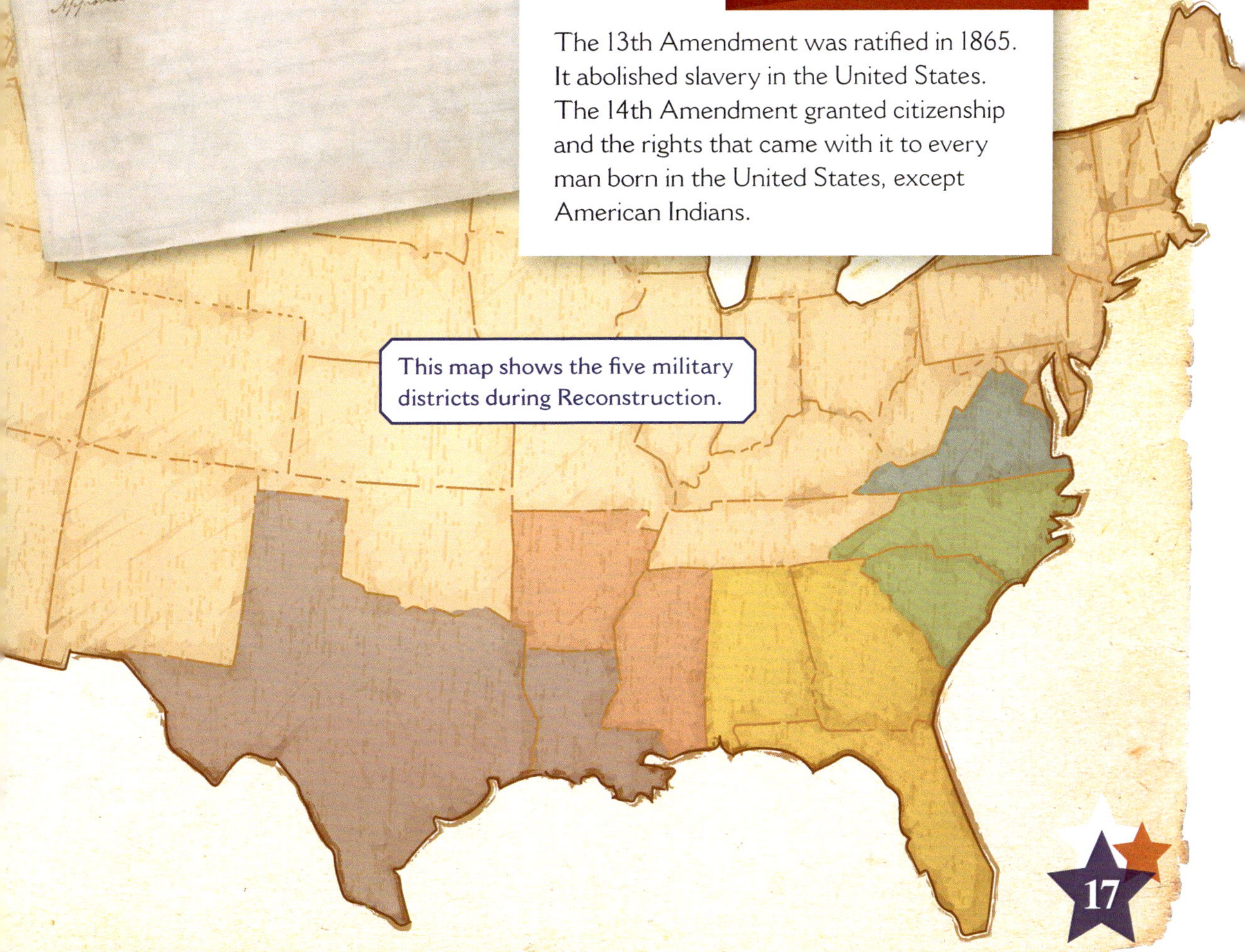

This map shows the five military districts during Reconstruction.

The Changing South

During the Reconstruction era, African Americans were allowed to vote in the South. They were also able to run for office. For the first time in history, they had a voice in government.

Many black **politicians** during this time had been born free. They knew how to read and write. They were often business owners or ministers. Some were teachers or farmers. They had no prior political experience, but they didn't let that stop them. They ran for office in state constitutional conventions that were taking place in the South. Many won seats in state **legislatures**. Some went all the way to Congress. Two African Americans were elected to the Senate, and 16 made it to the House of Representatives.

This 1867 illustration shows freedmen voting after being encouraged by carpetbaggers.

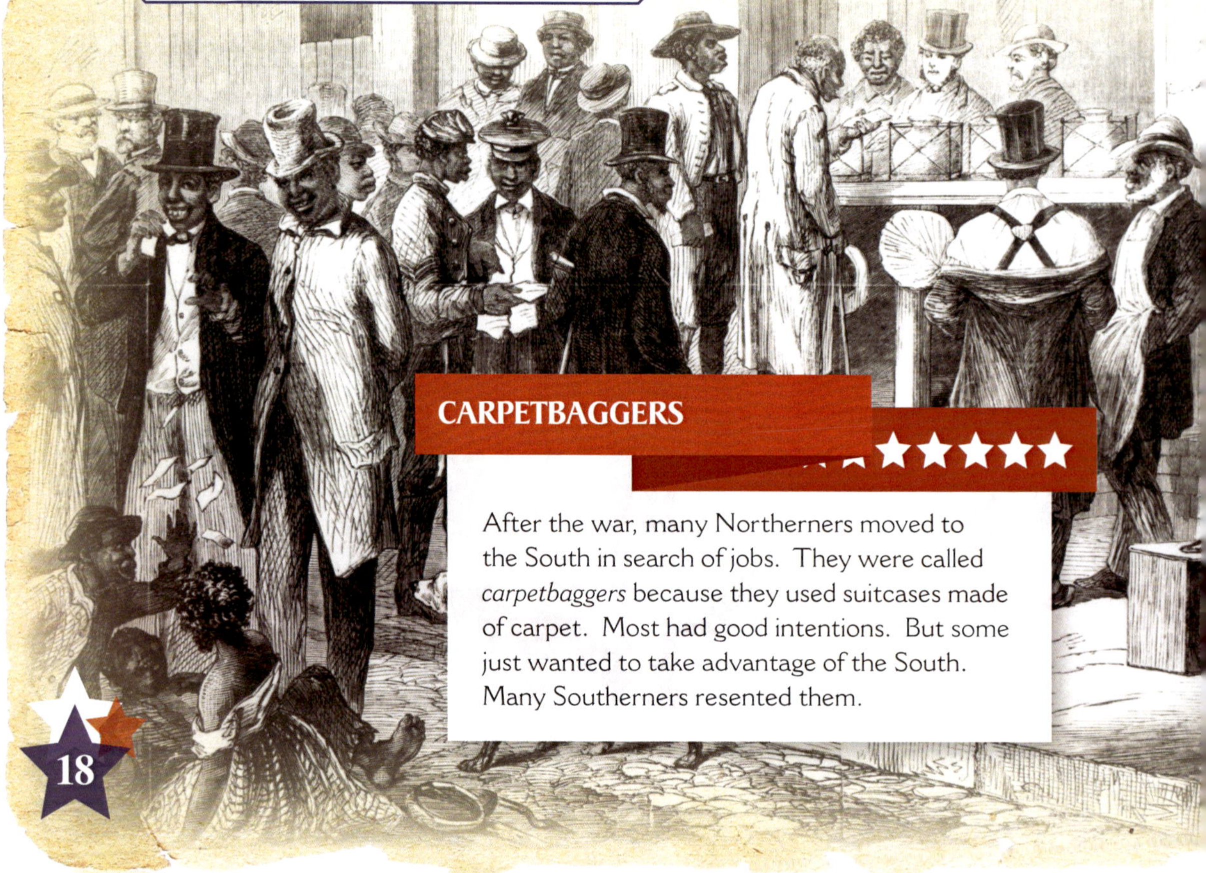

CARPETBAGGERS

After the war, many Northerners moved to the South in search of jobs. They were called *carpetbaggers* because they used suitcases made of carpet. Most had good intentions. But some just wanted to take advantage of the South. Many Southerners resented them.

Hiram Rhodes Revels was one of the two senators. He was elected in Mississippi in 1870. Revels was a preacher and a skilled speaker. This may have helped him get elected. During his time in the Senate, Revels backed **amnesty** for Southerners. He felt that as long as they pledged allegiance to the Union, they should be pardoned. He was against the separation of the races. He believed this increased hatred and fear among black people and white people. Tension between the two groups was on the rise.

Hiram Rhodes Revels

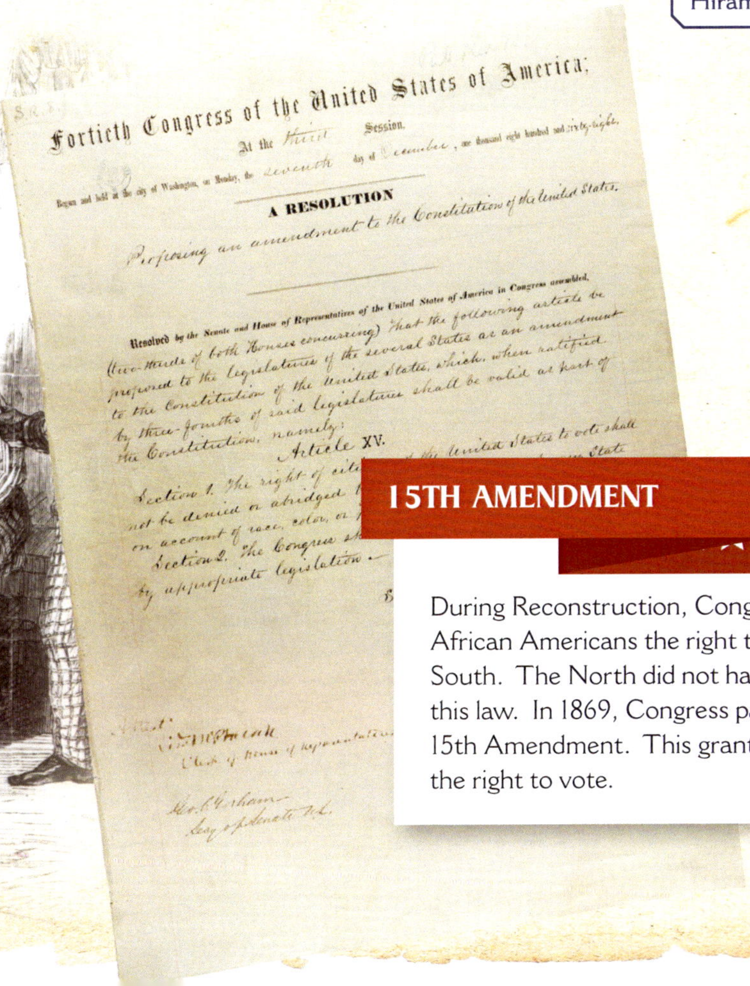

Fortieth Congress of the United States of America;

At the third Session,

Begun and held at the city of Washington, on Monday, the seventh day of December, one thousand eight hundred and sixty-eight.

A RESOLUTION

Proposing an amendment to the Constitution of the United States.

Resolved by the Senate and House of Representatives of the United States of America in Congress assembled, (two-thirds of both Houses concurring) That the following article be proposed to the legislatures of the several States as an amendment to the Constitution of the United States, which, when ratified by three-fourths of said legislatures shall be valid as part of the Constitution, namely:

Article XV.

Section 1. The right of citi[...] the United States to vote shall not be denied or abridged [...] State on account of race, color, or [...]

Section 2. The Congress sh[...] by appropriate legislation.

15TH AMENDMENT

During Reconstruction, Congress gave African Americans the right to vote in the South. The North did not have to follow this law. In 1869, Congress passed the 15th Amendment. This granted all men the right to vote.

Life in the South was changing quickly, and many white Southerners were not happy about it. Slavery had been abolished, black codes had been eliminated, and African Americans were voting and holding office. This enraged some Southerners. In response, they formed secret groups. These groups were made up of white **supremacists**. The most famous of these groups was the Ku Klux Klan.

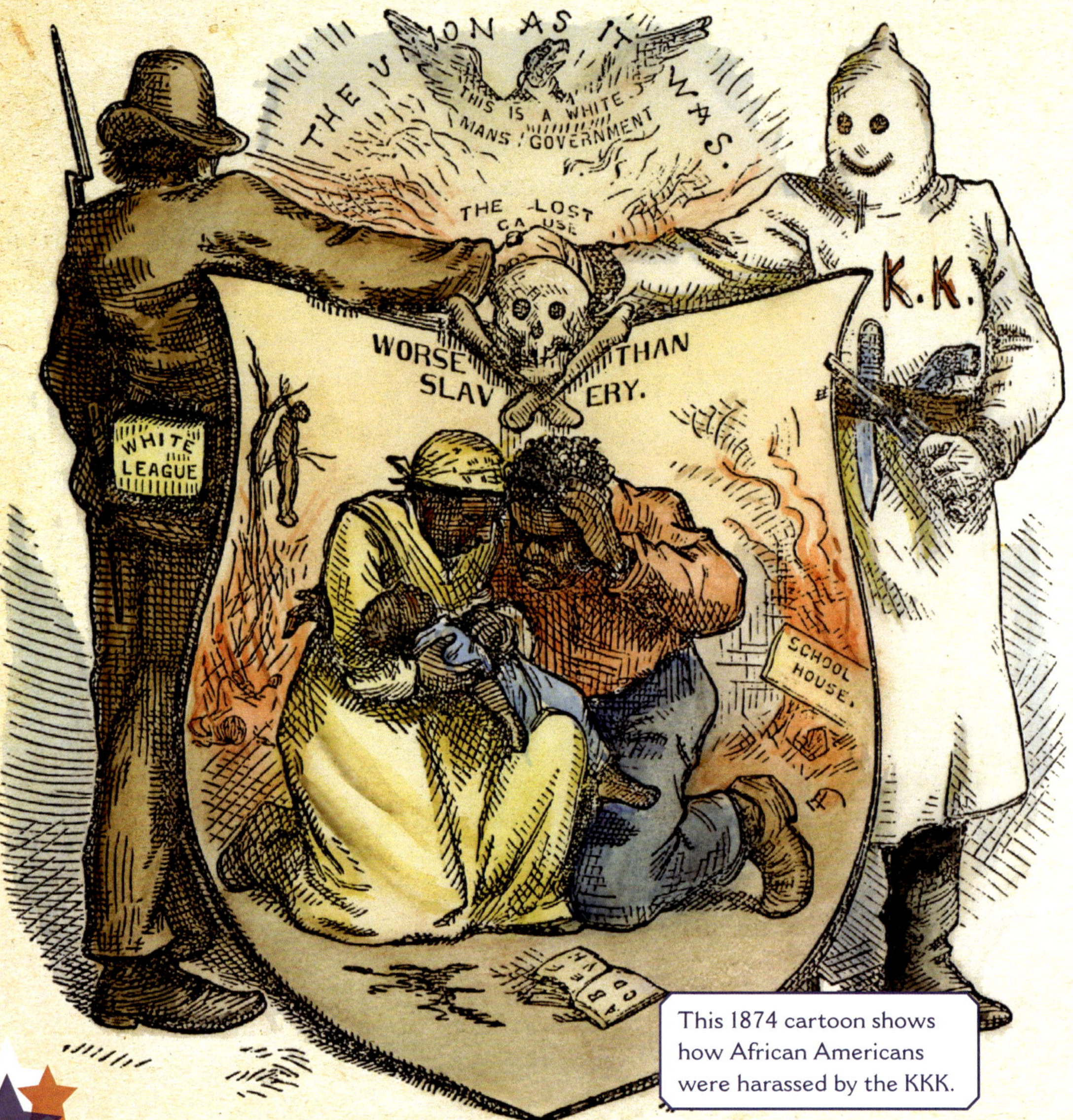

This 1874 cartoon shows how African Americans were harassed by the KKK.

Members of the Ku Klux Klan were not just former plantation owners. They were police officers and doctors. They were lawyers and mayors. Many white people, rich and poor, joined the hate group. Klan members were known to hide their identities with masks and costumes. They tried to intimidate African Americans. The Klan wanted to stop them from voting and buying houses. They did not want them to have jobs or run for office. If the bullying didn't work, they turned to violence. They viciously beat people to serve as a warning to others. The Klan even went so far as to kidnap and **lynch** African Americans. These groups soon became stronger than law enforcement. It was a terrifying time for African Americans.

Johnson receives news of his impeachment.

WHAT HAPPENED TO KING ANDY?

After President Johnson fired the secretary of war for siding with Congress, Congress **impeached** him. They charged him with improper behavior. His presidency was saved by one vote. But he was not reelected.

Ending Reconstruction

During Reconstruction, states were slowly admitted back into the Union. Georgia was the last state to rejoin in July of 1870. The Union was complete again. Yet, severe problems still plagued the nation.

In the South, racism and prejudice were a daily part of life. Violence was commonplace. There was still work to do, but support for Reconstruction began to decline. There was a **depression**. The **economy** was failing, and jobs were hard to find. Northerners were less concerned with issues in the South. They were now worried about money. They focused their attention on finding jobs and feeding their families. The government shifted its focus, too. The economy was now its main concern. Reconstruction was costly. So Congress began to remove troops from the South. Violence soared as a result, making it a more dangerous place for African Americans.

THE PANIC OF 1873

In the 1800s, the Jay Cooke and Company firm invested too much money in the building of railroads. They went bankrupt. This and many other factors sparked the Panic of 1873. During this time, people panicked as the country spiraled into an economic depression.

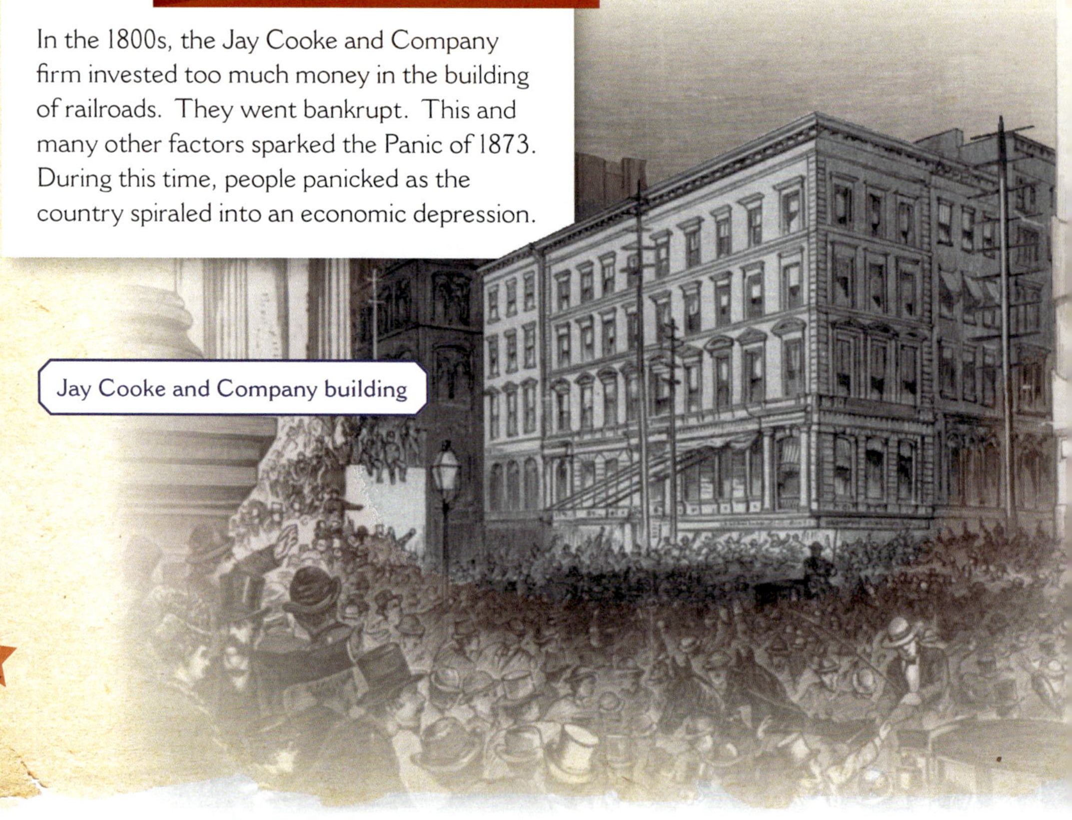

Jay Cooke and Company building

Congress did go on to pass the Civil Rights Act of 1875. It made **segregation** illegal. People of different races could not be separated in places such as theaters or restaurants. But, the law was rarely enforced. And when it was, African Americans often had a hard time proving their cases in white courts. In 1883, the Supreme Court ruled the law unconstitutional. It was thrown out. Segregation became the norm.

This image celebrates the Civil Rights Act of 1875.

The presidential election in 1876 was controversial. The Republican candidate was Rutherford B. Hayes. He ran against a Democrat, Samuel J. Tilden. After the election, the South declared that Tilden had won by a narrow margin. But, people thought that the votes were counted unfairly. Each side accused the other of fraud. Leaders from both parties met and came up with a compromise.

1876 campaign poster for Samuel J. Tilden

Rutherford B. Hayes

CHANGING PARTIES

The Democratic Party began to take shape in the 1820s. Its goal was to protect rural life. The Republican Party began in the 1850s. Republicans wanted to stop the spread of slavery. These parties still exist, and their goals have changed to reflect the times.

This 1874 cartoon depicts the Republican Party as an elephant, a symbol that is still used today.

The Compromise of 1877 was a promise between the Democrats and the Republicans. The Democrats agreed to let Hayes be president. But in return, he had to remove all troops from the South. This would end Reconstruction. He also had to appoint a Southerner to his cabinet and provide money for a new railroad in the South. Republicans had their own terms, too. They said Southern states had to respect the rights of African Americans. Both parties agreed to the terms. Hayes became the next president. Reconstruction was over.

A TRUCE—NOT A COMPROMISE, BUT A CHANCE FOR HIGH-TONED GENTLEMEN TO RETIRE GRACEFULLY FROM THEIR VERY CIVIL DECLARATIONS OF WAR.

This 1877 illustration symbolizes the Compromise of 1877.

Keep Moving Forward

The end of the Civil War and the abolishment of slavery gave hope to African Americans. There was a promise of a new life—one of freedom and equality. Reconstruction was the first step toward that dream. But in the end, it was not enough. There were small victories along the way. Yet, Reconstruction did not live up to its promise. The fight for civil rights would still be alive for decades to come. Segregation took a firm hold in the South. Violence and racism continued to haunt African Americans. Still, they boldly marched into the future.

African Americans kept fighting for their dreams. Booker T. Washington started a college for black students. W.E.B. DuBois earned his **doctorate** from Harvard and fought against racism. Thurgood Marshall, a lawyer who successfully argued against segregation in schools, became a **Supreme Court Justice**. Rosa Parks took a brave stance in the name of equality. And a man with a dream, Martin Luther King Jr., started a movement that ended with a new civil rights act. They fought hard. They never gave up. They kept moving forward.

W.E.B. DuBois

Thurgood Marshall

Booker T. Washington gives a speech in Mississippi.

In 1881, Booker T. Washington opened the Tuskegee Institute to educate African Americans.

Analyze It!

Think about the ways the U.S. government tried to rebuild and reunite the nation following the Civil War. Who was involved? What worked? What didn't work? Analyze the various plans and efforts that were used by government leaders. Then, create your own plan for Reconstruction. Use the parts that you feel worked, or create new ways to solve the issues the nation faced after the war. Create a slideshow presentation that explains your plan. Show how and why you think it will work better than those employed during the 1800s.

PRINTED BY
Entered according to act of Congress in the year 1871 by Th. Kelly in the Office of the Librarian of Congress at Washington D.C.
THOMAS KELLY 17 BARCLAY ST N.Y.
THE FIFTEENTH AMENDMENT
ncipation Proclamation
and Independence
Bonds of Fellowship.
of Rights the Holy Scriptures.
5 Education will prove the Equality the Races.
6 Liberty Protects the Mariage Alter.
7 Celebration of Fifteenth Amendment May 19th 1870
8 The Ballot Box is open to us.
9 Our representive Sits in the National Legislature
10 The Holy Ordinances of Religion are free
11 Freedom unites the Family Circle.
12 We will protect our Country as it defends our Rights.
13 We till our own Fields.
14 The Right of Citizens of the U.S. to vote shall not be denied or abridged by the U.S. or any State on account of Race Color or Condition of Servitude 15th Amendment

Glossary

amnesty—the decision that a group of people will not be punished

bureau—a department of the U.S. government

curfews—laws that require people to stay indoors after a certain time at night

depression—a period of time when many people do not have jobs and there is little money

doctorate—the highest degree given by a university

economy—the system of buying and selling goods and services

freedmen—formerly enslaved people who have been freed

impeached—charged a public official in office with a crime

legislatures—groups of people who have the authority to make laws

lynch—to be killed (usually by hanging) by a mob or group without legal authority

pardon—to officially excuse someone who is guilty of a crime without punishment

politicians—people who are active in government

prejudice—biased feelings against something or someone

racism—the belief that some races of people are superior over others

ratify—to make official by signing or voting

segregation—the practice of separating groups of people based on their race or religion

supremacists—people who believe that their race is superior to other races

Supreme Court Justice—a judge selected by the president to serve on the Supreme Court

tyrants—cruel and unfair rulers who have complete power and control over their countries

Union—term used to describe the United States of America; also the name given to the Northern army during the Civil War

vetoed—decided not to allow a new law to be passed

Index

Your Turn!

Political Cartoon

This 1874 political cartoon by Thomas Nast shows the South after the Civil War. In the cartoon, a black family huddles beneath members of two hate groups—the Ku Klux Klan and the White League. What do you think Nast wants his viewers to understand about the South after the Civil War? How do you know? Use sticky notes to annotate the cartoon and answer these questions.